spiritual encou

Sitting at the feet of Jesus

STEPHEN D & JACALYN EYRE

SCRIPTURE UNION

SCRIPTURE UNION
207-209 Queensway, Bletchley, Milton Keynes, MK2 2EB, England

---

First published in the United States by InterVarsity Press

First published in Great Britain by Scripture Union, 1995

Cover illustration: Brady Senior
Cover design: Mark Carpenter Design Consultants

ISBN 1 85999 020 7

Printed in England by Stanley L Hunt (Printers) Ltd, Midland Road, Rushden, Northants

Introducing Sitting at the Feet of Jesus

When we were first married, we decided that we wanted to build a bookcase that would function as a room divider, a TV and stereo stand and hold a few plants besides. We drew up a design and bought the lumber. However, it wasn't long before the project was in serious trouble. It wasn't that the bookcase was too ambitious, it was that we couldn't agree on how to go about building it.

Steve, being the man of the house and so forth, wanted to demonstrate his masculine prowess by his skillful use of wood and tools. There were several problems with approach—aside from the ego trip. First, Steve had never seen his father pick up a tool to build anything. That meant he was going to have to build the bookcase strictly by the book, without the benefit of any hands-on experience.

The second problem was that Jackie grew up in a house that her father built—while they were living in it. Jackie's dad first built the basement, making it a snug place to live. Then, coming home from work in the evenings, over a couple of years, he built on the first and second floors. The result was that Jackie has an ingrained understanding of building things and the use of tools. It wasn't until Steve was willing to acknowledge that Jackie had the greater experience and insight about building that the bookcase project moved ahead.

Learning from a book is great for some people, but it is no substitute for learning something from an experienced teacher. That is why Jesus, in his Great Commission, tells us to go out and make disciples. This is more than passing on information about Jesus to a new convert, it assumes that there will be a personal relationship involved in the education process.

The amazing thing about the Christian faith is that the discipleship relationship is not between the evangelist and the convert. The new disciple, by means of God's Word and Spirit, is able to enter into a discipleship relationship with the resurrected Lord Jesus Christ himself.

This guide has been written to be a means by which you can study the Sermon on the Mount in such in a way that you can personally talk with your Lord about his teaching. We are convinced that if you study the Lord's written Word and pay attention with your spiritual eyes and ears, that Jesus Christ himself will teach you.

Preparing to Sit at Jesus' Feet

The theme of the Sermon on the Mount is righteousness. It is more than how Jesus wants his disciples to act; it is how he wants them to be. Being righteous is not an easy idea to understand in a relativistic culture. Perhaps another way to say this is: "Being good is more than merely doing good things. Doing good things comes from a heart that is good."

The righteousness which Jesus expects of his disciples as it is revealed in his sermon is unsettling. Martin Luther wrote that it begins with "being poor in spirit because if you don't feel that way at the beginning of the Sermon you will certainly feel that way by the end." C. S. Lewis was once criticized for not caring for the Sermon on the Mount. He replied, "As to caring for, who likes being hit in the face with a sledge hammer and knocked flat?"

Living in a daily study of the Sermon for an extended period of time will be an unsettling experience, but a life-changing one. It is the extended application of what Jesus means by "Repent, the kingdom of heaven is at hand." The word *repent* means "a change of mind." And in the Sermon Jesus says explicitly what he means by a change of mind." The whole Sermon contrasts worldly ways of thinking and acting with godly ones.

This guide, following the outline of the Sermon, has four sections. The first part is an introduction, "Qualities of Discipleship." It covers three things: the Beatitudes, the salt-and-light effects of his disciples on others and Jesus' relationship to the Old Testament and with religious leaders.

The second section, "Righteous Relationships," covers Jesus' expectation of how his disciples should relate to others. Jesus teaches on murder, adultery and divorce, oaths, revenge and love.

The third section is "Righteous Acts and Attitudes." It covers charitable giving, prayer, fasting, desiring God and trusting him for our daily needs.

The final section, "Righteous Results," covers a number of topics that conclude the Sermon and encourage obedience by showing what results come from believing and obeying Christ.

Writing this guide was a team effort. In the introductions you'll read stories from Steve's experience, and in the study sections you'll see more of Jackie's hand.

Using the Guide

Some people think of a quiet time as being Bible study and prayer. We think of a quiet time as an opportunity to meet with God—in which you do Bible study and pray. The difference between the two definitions may seem small, but we think it is crucial. If a quiet time is just Bible study and prayer, then the relational dimension may easily get lost. You may end up merely going through the motions of religious activities and gaining some new information. However, if your goal is to set aside time to meet with God, then the whole dynamic of the quiet time is changed. It becomes a cultivation of a relationship and an opportunity for discipleship as the Lord meets with us.

Of course, because God's Word is his means of instructing us, we can't expect to learn from him unless we are spending serious time considering what has been written down for us. Likewise, prayer is the means by which we talk with him and ask for his help. But we must make sure that our prayer involves listening as well as asking. If we allow our prayer to degenerate into offering God a list of our desires and our recommendations for running the world, then we are no longer in a personal teacher-student relationship.

The format for each day in *Sitting at the Feet of Jesus,* as with all Spiritual Encounter Guides, includes five elements:

Introduction: This allows us to set the tone and introduce the day's issues for your quiet time.

Approach: This section is designed to help you to deal with mental and emotional obstacles that we all struggle with as we seek to shift our attention from ourselves to pay attention to God and his Word. Take some time with the approach question—five minutes or more. Use it to reach out to God so that you know you are meeting with him as you begin your study of his Word.

Study: These questions are written to help you focus on the content of the passage. They focus on the essential issues of each passage and on what they mean.

Reflect: In this section, we use the spiritual tools of silence and imagination to help you apply the passage to your soul and to life issues. Like the approach question, the more time you take with these questions, the more you will come away from your quiet time with a sense of personal encounter.

Pray: We offer a couple of suggestions for prayer. We expect during this time that you will develop your own prayer list as well. Take time to ask God for help and wisdom for yourself, your family, church, friends and whatever else you can think of. If you don't have a prayer list, you may find the chart at the back of the guide helpful.

Each quiet time will take you a minimum of twenty to thirty minutes, although you could easily spend more time if you work through the questions in a leisurely, reflective manner.

Approach	Study
Reflect	Pray

How to Think About Quiet Time

A word of caution: this guide is not intended to make you feel guilty. It's a funny thing, but in our experience, people who don't have quiet times don't feel much guilt about it. On the other hand, people who think that quiet times are important often experience a good deal of guilt. It seems that the expectation on the part of many people is that you must have one every day or else you will be a spiritual failure. Quiet time guides can nourish this inclination because it is obvious when it has been a couple days since you last used the guide. Of course, this guilt feeds on itself and after a while you avoid the guide altogether because you don't want to confront your sense of failure.

We like the advice that Brother Lawrence gave in *The Practice of the Presence of God.* He wrote that he never condemned himself for missing the mark in his times with God. He knew that God was not surprised at his "failure"; instead, he knew that God was delighted whenever he took time to pray. After all, God is not a petulant father who scolds us when we don't write home. If you follow his example, you will discover that you will choose to meet with God, not because you have to but because you desire to.

In order to keep this guide from being a "guilt producer" we have not divided it by weeks. Instead, we have merely numbered the days. Some weeks you may have a quiet time six out of seven days. That's great! Other weeks you may have only one or two. That's still great! God doesn't love you more on the weeks that you have a quiet time every day or less on the weeks when you have no quiet time at all. God loves you through the free grace given to you by faith in Jesus Christ.

Learning to Live Right

We lived in England for a couple of years. Learning to drive there required a mental revolution. Changing sides of the road went against twenty years of driving experience in the U.S. Doing what seemed natural, driving on the right, was wrong. Doing what felt wrong, driving on the left, was right.

When Jesus calls us to himself, we too must learn a new way of thinking. That which seems natural to us through years of learned patterns of thought and behavior no longer fits the demands of the king. In spending time in the Sermon on the Mount, you are going to struggle with days when it won't seem like you are doing so well. But if you keep at it, then you will find that new thought patterns and actions will take over your life. That's what sitting at the feet of Jesus is all about.

PART 1 *Qualities of Discipleship*

DAY 1

The Lord's Attention

Matthew 4:23—5:2

Yet I am always with you;
you hold me by my right hand.
You guide me with your counsel,
and afterward you will take me into glory. (Ps 73:23-24)

Sunday morning worship is important to me. I love being surrounded by people who sing hymns in a heartfelt way and who pray as if they believed that their lives depend on it. On most Sundays I come away uplifted and refreshed.

But I have found that Sundays are not enough. I need personal time with God as well. I need to know that he knows my name and is involved in the details of my life. I need his personal guidance.

Peter, Andrew, James, John and the other disciples must have had the same need as well. After being with the crowds, Jesus often took them aside for personal attention and private instruction. In the Sermon on the Mount we have the most complete and concise summary of Jesus' direct teaching of his disciples.

The good news is that such personal instruction is not limited to the first disciples. It is available to his disciples in every generation. It is available to you and me. All that is required is that we read, listen and respond.

Approach

Someone once commented, "God doesn't have favorites but he does have intimates." Write a couple of sentences to God telling him that you want to be close to him and know him better.

Study

1. Read Matthew 4:23—5:2. News about Jesus spread throughout Galilee as he began his ministry. What was Jesus doing and saying to collect such crowds (4:23-24)?

2. In a large crowd like the one Matthew describes, what would be some of the reasons for seeking Jesus?

3. Consider other significant events related to mountains in the Scriptures. Look up the following passages and write down a summary of each one:

Exodus 19:20—20:1

1 Kings 19:11-13a

Matthew 17:1-7

Acts 1:10-12

What might be the significance of Jesus teaching on a mountain?

4. Why do you think Jesus focused on his disciples rather than the crowd?

Reflect

1. What would it be like to be following Jesus among the crowds? Write down what you might feel emotionally and physically, and what you might hear and say to others.

2. Just as Jesus called the disciples out from the crowd to teach them, Jesus wants to give you the same personal attention. How prepared would you be to listen if Jesus called you out from the crowd to receive his personal instruction?

3. Write down the hindrances to being a disciple that you find in your heart and turn them over to the Lord.

Pray

Ask God to give you the attitude of a disciple, with a listening ear and a responsive heart.

Pray that Jesus' kingdom would continue to expand and that many would hear his Word and receive his healing touch.

DAY 2

Needy People

Matthew 5:3-6

When you eat and are satisfied, be careful that you do not forget the LORD who brought you out of Egypt, out of the land of slavery. (Deut 6:11-12)

I hate being dependent upon others.

When I was small I didn't call on my older brothers to help me with bullies in the neighborhood. When there was sickness and death in my family, as a young boy, I took pride in not looking to others for comfort. I wanted to be able to handle life on my own.

I became a Christian when I was eighteen as my determined self-dependence began to falter in the face of the pressures of life. Despite my walls of resistance, I came face-to-face with my need for God.

During the first years of my Christian walk, I enjoyed the good things God did for me. I learned and grew a lot. But then I thought that I was ready to take it on my own. "Stand back, God, I'll take it from here."

Much to my dismay, I discovered that being a disciple of Jesus didn't work that way. When I marched off on my own, the Lord had a way of allowing the rug to slip out from under me. Jesus didn't say, "Blessed are those who *were* poor in spirit." He said, "Blessed are those who *are* poor in spirit." Being dependent upon God is a way of life, every day, every minute. It is to those who know their continuing spiritual poverty that the riches of his kingdom are an inexhaustible resource.

Approach

Set aside the illusion that you have anything to offer to God that he needs. Set aside the things you own which nourish your sense of spiritual independence. Sit quietly until you are aware of your need for God.

Study

1. Read Matthew 5:3-6. Jesus announces that those who have the special attention of God don't fit the world's standards of privileged people. Write out what you think each means. (Use a dictionary to help you. Write out the definition in your own words.)

Poor:

Mourn:

Meek:

Hunger and thirst:

2. Poverty, mourning, meekness and hunger and thirst are conditions we naturally seek to avoid. Why?

3. What might the first disciples have felt when they heard Jesus teach these things?

4. How does Jesus' teaching transform these "negative" conditions in a beneficial way?

Reflect

1. These traits on which Jesus pronounces a blessing are in direct contrast to what our culture considers as characteristics of privileged people. How do you feel knowing that Jesus values these conditions?

2. When in your life have you especially felt your need for God?

3. What was your relationship to the Lord like during times of personal loss or serious life stress?

4. You don't need life crises to live in the state of dependence which Jesus blesses. Write out reasons why you need him on a daily basis.

Pray

See yourself as empty of spiritual resources and in serious need of God's help. Spend time calling out for God to fill you with his righteousness and give you the riches of his Spirit.

Mourn over the rebellious condition of this world, and ask God to bring his righteousness to those who are deprived of justice.

DAY 3

Blessed People
Matthew 5:3-6

Wait for the LORD
and keep his way.
He will exalt you to inherit the land. (Ps 37:34)

Administration is not one of my gifts. This is not an easy thing for me to admit. For one thing, not being good at administration means that details are always falling through the cracks. For another, everyone knows that to be successful in our day you have to be good at making programs work. Somehow I feel as if I am not up to standard. Of course, if I had the gift of administration, I would probably discover that I was lacking in some other area that was "essential."

Limits are a part of life. Sometimes we face limits that are part of our personality, sometimes we face limits that come from the circumstances of life. Whatever our limitations they are threatening to us because we have an inner need not to be needy. We work to have enough money so that we won't be dependent upon others. Likewise, we evaluate and adjust our personalities so that we can be smiling, attractive people.

However much we work to overcome our limitations, there will be more to life than we can competently handle. We can either become driven and hardened people who refuse to face the limitations of life. Or, we can become responsive and open people who know that even our limitations are gifts.

Our needs and limitations, honestly faced, force us to look for help. And when we look, God is there eagerly waiting to meet us.

Approach

Consider the limitations of life that you are facing. Write them down. Sit quietly looking for God to come to you in your needs.

Study

1. Read Matthew 5:3-6. The word *blessed* is sometimes translated as *happy*. But that doesn't quite get at the idea. Blessed means "divine favor" or "receiving special attention from God." Write out in your own words what the blessing is for each need.

Spiritual poverty:

Mourn:

Meek:

Hunger and thirst for righteousness:

2. Considering each state of need, why is the word *happy* insufficient to describe the result of God meeting each one?

3. What do you learn about God from the specific blessings that he brings to each need?

Reflect

1. Each of these conditions implies a deficit, each blessing brings a way to fill it up. Make a list of major losses in your life. Instead of seeking to avoid pain, allow God to come to you in comfort. As you write, record how you feel. (You will probably need to use a sheet of paper.)

2. Freedom from guilt and shame is a condition that can't be achieved by human effort. Ask God to fill you up with righteousness by washing away your sense of sin and guilt. Choose to see God pouring righteousness into you and sit for a while in a quiet attitude of reception. Write down your perceptions and impressions.

Pray

Ask God to spread a spirit of dependence throughout your church.

Pray for those you know who are experiencing a loss, perhaps of health, of a loved one or a job. Ask God to give them the strength to hurt, the courage to mourn and the openness to receive God's comfort.

DAY 4

Gracious People

Matthew 5:7-12

Do not let any unwholesome talk come out of your mouths, but only what is helpful for building others up according to their needs, that it may benefit those who listen. . . . Be kind and compassionate to one another, forgiving each other, just as in Christ God forgave you. (Eph 4:29, 32)

Last week I overstepped my bounds. In a conversation in a hallway I made some comments about the quality of leadership of a fellow pastor. Not quite put-downs you understand. But I spoke with a mutual friend in such a way as to indicate that perhaps I had the edge in dealing with the subject of an upcoming conference that he (not I) was responsible for. And, of course, just after I made the comment my colleague rounded the corner.

My heart hit the floor. There was no way to know whether he had overheard any of the conversation. Certainly, he gave no indication that he had. But I was embarrassed. All through the next day it gnawed at me. I knew I was out of line. I was in several meetings with him and nothing was said. But I couldn't relax. I knew my attitude and conversation were not conducive to building trust.

And so, I made a visit to his office. I apologized and asked for forgiveness. Without a moment's hesitation he said: "I know what it's like to be tempted to put yourself ahead of others. I accept your apology. Thanks for your honesty."

I walked out of the office grateful for his grace. The unsettling sense of guilt was gone, as was the guarded sense of distance. The partnership that we were building could continue despite my self-aggrandizement.

Forgiving people opens doors that otherwise stay closed. Christian discipleship is a lifestyle of forgiving and needing to be forgiven. Several times throughout the rest of the Sermon on the Mount Jesus is going to raise the issue. This quiet time today just opens the door.

Approach

Those who forgive are those who know they are forgiven. Spend time in quiet appreciation of the affectionate forgiveness that Jesus Christ constantly brings into your life. Write down what it feels like to be forgiven by God.

Study

1. Read Matthew 5:7-12. These beatitudes have a different focus from the preceding ones. They prescribe how Jesus wants his disciples to relate to others. In your own words give a definition of each one.

Merciful:

Pure in heart:

Peacemakers:

2. In your own words, describe a person who is merciful, pure in heart and a peacemaker.

3. Considering verses 10 and 11, living by the Beatitudes is not a recipe for winning a popularity contest. How is it that living by the Beatitudes could bring persecution?

Reflect

1. Jesus wants us to be merciful. Recall a time when you were offended or hurt by a friend, family member or someone from your church. Write down what happened, how you were hurt and how you felt about it.

2. Consider how your relationship with that person is today. If you were able to extend healing mercy, thank God for his work in you. If you were not merciful, ask God what he needs to do in you so that you can extend mercy. Write down what you sense God may be saying to you.

3. Peacemakers are those who encourage people to extend mercy to each other. Consider relationships in your family and/or church. In what ways might the Lord want you to function as a peacemaker?

4. Someone who is pure in heart doesn't have deceitful motives toward others. Ask God to do some purifying in you. Imagine your heart as a house with closets full of mixed motives. Ask God to walk through the house, opening doors and bringing out into the open hidden motives that might be hurtful to others. After a time of allowing God to work, write down what comes to mind.

5. Now turn over each item you have written down and ask God to take them from you.

Pray
Ask God to bring peace in your relationships in every area of your life.

Pray for your church, ask God to work mercy, purity of heart and peacemaking into all relationships.

Pray for those who have had the courage to stand up for righteousness and are paying a price for it.

DAY 5

Privileged People

Matthew 5:7-12

Now we see but a poor reflection as in a mirror;
then we shall see face to face.
Now I know in part; then I shall know fully,
even as I am fully known. (1 Cor 13:12)

This morning before school I took my eight-year-old out for a Coke and a Danish at the local McDonald's. I haven't been around much lately because of a busy schedule. He wasn't complaining, but my wife said she could see that my absence was taking its toll.

We didn't talk about anything notable or significant. I drank coffee, and we looked over some of his spelling words. We had ten minutes together, and then it was time to go. I pulled up in front of the school, tousled his hair and said goodby. With a squeeze of the hand and "Thanks, Dad," he was out the door of the car and up the steps and into the school building. The time could have been longer and our conversation more significant. But it was good just to be together.

Like my sons, I need the personal attention of my heavenly Father. I don't always have to seek him for pressing needs, I just need to know that I am important to him. The good news is that not only does Jesus bestow his personal attention on his disciples as he teaches them, he promises the personal attention of his heavenly father as well.

Approach

Sit quietly in the presence of God. Talk with him about what is on your mind, not necessarily for the sake of getting him to fix a problem or give you wisdom. Spend a few minutes with him merely because you want to be with him. After a time of quiet write down what it was like.

Study

1. Read Matthew 5:7-12. To see just how important each blessing is, write down what the opposite of each character trait is.
They will be shown mercy:

See God:

Called sons of God:

Given the kingdom of heaven:

2. Jesus uses the present and future tense in each beatitude. "Blessed are . . . because they shall . . ." What is present about each blessing, and what do we have to wait for in the future?

Reflect

1. One day we shall see God face to face. Write down what you think that will feel like. (Remember that you won't feel guilty, because of his mercy promised in verse 7 and the righteousness he gives [v. 6].)

2. Consider that you will be called a child of God and given the rights and freedoms of his kingdom. Imagine that you have arrived and are being proclaimed before the court of heaven. What will it be like?

3. Knowing this is a firm and certain promise to those who are Jesus' obedient disciples, what differences can it make in the way you face the pressures of this week?

4. Some of our struggles come because life is difficult. However, some of our struggles come because of intentional opposition to our relationship to Jesus Christ. When have you ever experienced opposition from other people?

How did it affect you?

Pray

Pray for those Christians who are experiencing resistance and persecution for their faith.

Spend time in thanksgiving for the future that awaits you in Jesus Christ.

DAY 6

Significant People

Matthew 5:13-16

I will make you into a great nation
and I will bless you;
I will make your name great,
and you will be a blessing . . .
and all peoples on earth
will be blessed through you. (Gen 12:2-3)

Bob Dylan, the prophet of the 1960s, heralded changing times, as Scott Mackenzie wrote, "a whole generation with a new explanation," new values, new political programs and the hope of universal peace. In the Age of Aquarius, baby boomers left the church in record numbers as the church was thought to stand for outdated truth and outdated morality.

However, the hoped-for new day didn't turn out as expected. Drug trips didn't take you anywhere other than to fantasyland and personal nightmares. The boomers graduated from college, climbed the career ladder, and had families. Life went on, but something was missing. Instead of making a significant impact on society, many began to struggle with a sense of personal significance.

Now large numbers of those baby boomers who left the church, about one-half, are returning. Surveys show they seek a sense of personal significance and religious education for their children. They come seeking something more than what the world offers.

For 2,000 years Jesus Christ has been making disciples who have something more to offer. His disciples know they are personally significant. They also know that they have a world-changing agenda.

Approach

Our sense of significance is often enhanced or decreased by others who pay attention to us as well as by the number of our responsibilities. Sit quietly in the Lord's presence. Ask why you are important to him. Write down what comes to mind.

Study

1. Read Matthew 5:13-16. Jesus uses two images to describe the impact his disciples will have on the world—salt and light. Evidently, what was used for salt at that time was a combination of sodium chloride mixed with sand and other impurities. The sodium chloride could be leached out leaving only the impurities. How are these images of salt and light both encouraging and challenging?

2. What do these images imply about the impact Jesus was expecting on the world through his disciples?

Life Without Refrigeration	**Your Family Without Christian Influence**

3. Look back over the Beatitudes (all the verses that begin with "blessed"). How is it that the people Jesus describes in the Beatitudes can have such a significant impact on the world?

4. What pressures do disciples face that would cause us to hide our lights?

Reflect

1. In many ways Christianity has been on the defensive in Western culture for the past couple hundred years. For example, in the college classroom we may hear how oppressive the church was in the Middle Ages, or how unfair the Crusades were. Much of the criticism is well deserved. But the fault of Christians through the ages is not the whole story. In what ways have Christians functioned as salt and light in the world?

2. One of the functions of salt before the invention of refrigeration was preservation. Let's be creative. Consider how different your life would be if you didn't have a refrigerator. Then consider how your family might be different if you weren't a Christian.

Pray

Ask God to work in your family to show you godly ways to live.

Ask God to work through your church to make it salt and light in your community.

DAY 7

Righteous People

Matthew 5:17-20

Give me understanding, and I will keep your law and obey it with all my heart. (Ps 119:34)

In a book entitled *The Intellectuals*, Paul Johnson writes that within the past two hundred years we have been living in a period defined by a group of audacious revolutionaries. Describing the new age they were bringing in as "the Enlightenment," these revolutionaries set aside the teachings of both the religious leaders and the philosophers of the preceding centuries. Based on human reason and hard work, intellectuals such as Rousseau and Voltaire, Marx and Nietzsche, were convinced that they could construct a utopia. These men were audacious, Johnson writes, because their claims to come up with original insights, divorced from thinkers of the past, had never been attempted by other thinkers in any other period of world history.

In contrast to the thinkers of the Enlightenment, Jesus, who had the authority of God and whose teachings were revolutionary, did not set aside the teaching of the priests, prophets and scribes who went before him. He saw his ministry as a means not to eradicate the Old Testament, but to fulfill it. In the ministry of Jesus there is a continuity with God's work in the past.

The followers of Jesus, therefore, are not to dismiss what came before him but to live in fulfilled obedience to all of God's Word.

Approach

You don't know enough to run your life in a way that will enable you to meet all challenges that come your way. Jot down the problems you are presently facing. After each one write "I need to be shown what I should do; I don't know." After you have done this, sit quietly for a while in the rest that comes from not having to be omni-competent or omniscient.

Study

1. Read Matthew 5:17-20. There are those who feel that the Old Testament is no longer relevant for Christians. Based on your reading of this passage, what do you think Jesus would say?

2. Jesus makes a distinction between *abolishing* and *fulfilling* the Law. How can the distinction between those two words help us understand a Christian's relationship to the Old Testament?

3. According to Jesus, how is a person's spiritual status related to obeying the commandments?

4. The Pharisees were the most meticulous people of the day for keeping the Law. How do you think the disciples felt when they heard that the requirements of the kingdom were even more demanding?

Reflect

1. We are to *practice* keeping the commandments. This takes effort. Measure your behavior this past week or two against the Beatitudes. Note where you measured up and where you fell short.

Blessed are the poor in spirit:

Blessed are those who mourn:

Blessed are the meek:

Blessed are those who hunger and thirst after righteousness:

Blessed are the merciful:

Blessed are the pure in heart:

Blessed are the peacemakers:

2. Because we all fall short, our only hope of entering the kingdom of heaven comes as a free gift to us by faith in Jesus Christ. In quiet reflection lay your sins at the foot of the cross and see God give you his forgiveness. Write down your inner responses.

Pray

Thank God for the gift of his Word in the Old and New Testaments.

Pray that you will hunger and thirst for righteousness.

PART 2 *Righteous Relationships*

DAY 8

Anger

Matthew 5:21-22

"Teacher, which is the greatest commandment in the Law?" Jesus replied: " 'Love the Lord your God with all your heart and with all your soul and with all your mind.' This is the first and greatest commandment. And the second is like it: 'Love your neighbor as yourself.' All the Law and the Prophets hang on these two commandments." (Mt 22:36-40)

Picture a little old lady standing over her grandchildren as they squabble. While the disagreement grows in intensity, the elderly woman stands by wringing her hands saying, "Now children be nice to one another; let's get along." As a boy, that was my impression of Christianity. Christianity seemed to me to be not so much about knowing God, but rather an anemic urging to be kind to one another.

After a life-changing personal encounter with God when I was eighteen, I learned a great deal about the Bible and a great deal about God. But very little was said about right relationships. What came across to me in the teaching I got was that God wasn't really interested in how we treated each other, as long as we believed properly.

Looking back, I believe that both emphases were off-balance. Christianity has a horizontal and a vertical dimension. One is inseparable from the other. The first table of the law is about the worship of God; the second table of the law is about right relationships. In his instructions to his disciples, Jesus powerfully brings the human heart before God in the midst of relationships with each other.

Approach

Right relationships with God and others grow directly from the certain conviction that God loves you. Before you begin your study today spend time resting in the fatherly care of God for you. Write down your impressions of being held in his care.

Study

1. Jesus begins his instruction on fulfilling the Law by teaching with the sixth commandment, "You shall not murder." What other expressions of social hostility does he mention besides murder?

2. Why is Jesus placing anger, a hostile emotional response, on par with murder, an act of physical violence?

3. Jesus also soundly rebukes acts of verbal violence, saying, "Raca" (the Aramaic equivalent of "idiot") and calling someone a "fool." Why?

4. What effect do you think that this teaching would have had on the disciples and the others who were listening to him?

Reflect

1. Jesus' handling of the Law makes it more penetrating and comprehensive. Few of us are murderers, although almost all of us have spoken verbally abusive language at some time, and all of us are guilty of personal animosity. Make a list of times in recent memory when you were angry and/or verbally abusive. As you do, write down the source of your anger, the intensity of your anger and the way you handled your anger.

Source of Anger	Intensity of Anger	Way You Handled Anger

2. Instead of making excuses for your anger, choose to admit your guilt according to the teaching of Jesus and ask him to forgive and cleanse you. In a time of reflection tell him how you feel and how you struggle with anger. Write down how you perceive him responding to you.

3. Anger often comes from a sense of being hurt or offended. In order to get beyond our anger we need to forgive. Who do you need to forgive?

Sit quietly in God's presence asking him to show you who you need to forgive and to give you the spiritual power to forgive.

4. What difference will living according to Jesus' instruction on anger make in the way you live?

Pray

Ask God to touch each person you listed in the reflection time with his love and grace.

Ask God to apply Jesus' teaching to those in your church or Christian fellowship.

DAY 9

Reconciliation

Matthew 5:23-26

How good and pleasant it is
when brothers live together in unity! (Ps 133:1)

This past winter I was flying out to California to lead a conference on meditative prayer. On the plane, as I was praying for the weekend, I grew painfully aware that Bob, a ministry colleague, was angry with me. I knew that there had been a growing tension, but I had not taken the initiative or time to deal with it. Besides, I hate conflict.

The more I tried to shake off this awareness of Bob's anger, the more uncomfortable I became. Every time I tried to focus on my preparation the issue of Bob became more pressing. Before I could do anything with a sense of spiritual integrity, I found that I needed to make a determined effort to seek Bob out as soon as I returned home.

Sitting on my desk when I arrived back in my office the following week was a letter from Bob. I was surprised. I was not surprised, however, to read that in fact he was angry with me. I was relieved to read that he was writing to apologize for his anger and to seek my forgiveness.

I wrote back with an acceptance and an apology of my own. That led to a phone call a couple of days later, and that in turn led to a renewed relationship of open communication.

Jesus wants his followers to have life-sustaining relationships with each other. When we draw close to him, he directs us to do whatever is necessary to remove offenses that we give and receive.

Approach

As you begin your quiet time today, listen to the voices in your head which are expressing your pressing concerns. Write down each "voice." Imagine each one as a phone call that you need to share with the Lord. Answer them all and transfer them to him until all the lights on the switchboard have stopped blinking and you have a sense of inner quiet.

Study

1. Read Matthew 5:23-26. In his continuing explanation of the sixth commandment, Jesus shifts the focus from anger inside us to anger directed at us. Describe what Jesus wants his disciples to do in the two incidents of conflict he mentions.

2. It is not possible to tell who is the guilty party in either the religious context (vv. 23-24) or the civil context (vv. 25-26). What can we learn from this about Jesus' expectations for reconciliation?

3. Read through the Beatitudes (vv. 3-10) again. How does Jesus' instruction here apply his teaching in the Beatitudes?

4. Consider all the verses in this section from the studies yesterday and today (vv. 21-26). Summarize Jesus' teaching on personal conflict.

Reflect

1. Seeking reconciliation with someone who is angry with you often doesn't feel good and may not seem fair. Why not?

2. What difference would this make in your church if Jesus' teaching on reconciliation were diligently applied?

3. Spend some time worshiping God. If people come to mind that have something against you, write down their names so that you can make plans to get matters reconciled.

Pray

Ask God to prepare the way for you in the heart(s) of the people you need to talk to as you seek reconciliation.

Pray that your church or Christian fellowship would be a place of reconciliation.

DAY 10

Lust

Matthew 5:27-30

Can a man walk on hot coals
without his feet being scorched?
So is he who sleeps with another man's wife;
no one who touches her will go unpunished. (Prov 6:28-29)

Neither of us has committed adultery. However, there is something that does seem rather romantic about it. The hidden secrets, the attraction, the desire, the anticipation, the forbidden fruit. . . .

I think such adulterous adventures would look particularly inviting if someone was bored with the routines of life, or perhaps lonely because of a workaholic partner. Or perhaps, if a marriage was full of stress and fighting.

The romance of illicit love however pales against the cost of such adventures. Looking each other in the eye with a trusting glance, the confidence of commitment to each other that transcends boredom or other pressures—these are the benefits of faithfulness.

In a culture that is content with commitments of convenience—"I'll be faithful as long as it is to my advantage"—the trusting confidence of a Christian marriage is rare. As disciples of Jesus, in the face of the pressure from our secularizing culture, we need to look again at Jesus' teaching on marriage with the eternal perspective he provides.

Approach

God has promised, "I will never leave you nor forsake you." Because of this we need not live in fear of rejection from him. Write down the pressures of life you face and consider them in the light of God's never-changing eternal commitment to you.

Study

1. Read Matthew 5:27-30. Although Jesus teaches on adultery and divorce here, what can you discern about his perspective on marriage from these verses?

2. How does Jesus redefine the definition of adultery?

3. Describe Jesus' attitude toward sin.

Reflect

1. What are your own feelings and reactions to Jesus' teaching on adultery?

2. Why do you think Jesus' teaching on marriage and sexuality is so severe?

3. Sinful actions flow from sinful thoughts. When have your thoughts paved the way for disobedience to God in some aspect (not only your sexuality) of your life?

4. How have you been affected, directly or indirectly, by lust or sexual immorality?

5. Lust is an inordinately strong desire for another person. Picture your strong desires as raging dragons. Take several minutes to take them before God. Ask him to transform them into a strong desire for him. Write down what happens.

Pray

Pray for new understanding of the seriousness of sin and the magnitude of sin and Jesus' redemption on the cross.

Pray for those friends or relatives who might be entangled in an extramarital affair. (Perhaps you may need to seek God for yourself in this area as well.) Ask God to bring conviction and deliverance.

DAY 11

M*arriage*

Matthew 5:31-32

I have loved you with an everlasting love;
I have drawn you with loving-kindness. (Jer 31:3)

I hate to admit it but I was relieved when Lynn's first marriage was over. Her husband was an immature and selfish man who caused heartache and pain for Lynn and her two boys for years. Yet, I believe that divorce is wrong. It is a tragedy that tears the fabric of the soul and leaves scars for a lifetime. However, Lynn's abusive marriage was also a tragedy that was doing damage that would last a lifetime.

In struggling through this issue of divorce, I have come to see that Jesus closes the door on those who want to give up on marriage when the going gets tough. However, as you read today's passage, you will see that our Lord doesn't completely close the door. He leaves it open just a crack. Knowing when it's closed and when it's open is an important and difficult task that his followers need to ponder.

Approach

"God with us" is the promise and the blessing of the Christian faith. Think back over the past week. In what ways has God shown his presence and his care for you?

Once you've made your notes, sit back and enjoy just being with him.

Study

1. Read Matthew 5:31-32. Jesus is comparing their current practice of divorce with God's law. In your own words, what is he saying?

2. The practice of divorce in Jesus' time allowed the male to divorce at his whim while making the female responsible for not pleasing him. How does Jesus confront this hypocrisy?

3. Jesus allows for divorce when there has been "marital unfaithfulness." What actions and attitudes could come under that definition?

Reflect

1. What are the essential elements of a good marriage?

2. How would our society be different if people lived by Jesus' teaching?

3. Just as lust is an inappropriately strong desire for a person, wanting a divorce is an inappropriately strong desire turned against a person. Picture your desires against another person, your spouse or someone else, as a raging dragon. Take it before God and ask him to transform it. Write down what happens.

Pray

Pray for your relationship to God, that you would draw closer and more intimate with him.

Pray for the marriages of Christian couples, that God would strengthen and enrich them.

DAY 12

Commitment

Matthew 5:33-37

My soul finds rest in God alone;
my salvation comes from him.
He alone is my rock and my salvation;
he is my fortress, I will never be shaken. (Ps 62:1-2)

Relationships are built on trust. It's dangerous to do business with a person who won't keep commitments. Likewise, it's dangerous to share friendship with people who may later use parts of your conversation to your cost and their advantage.

I'm not quite comfortable with the phrase "I'll be honest with you." It makes me wonder how honest the speaker was in the other parts of our conversation that weren't prefaced with this commitment to honesty.

In a British book on understanding American culture the following joke offers painful social commentary:

Question: "What's 'Californian' for 'boy am I ever gonna screw you up'?"

Answer: "Trust me, trust me."

In the passage today Jesus addresses the issue of the integrity of the words of his disciples.

Approach
God keeps his commitments to us. Write down all the ways that God has kept his commitment to you for your daily needs of food, shelter and daily necessities.

How does this apply to the anxieties that you are currently coping with?

Study
1. Read Matthew 5:33-37. In verse 33, Jesus teaches concerning oaths. What have the disciples been taught about oaths in the past?

2. What reasons does Jesus give for not swearing by heaven, by earth . . . or anything else?

3. This teaching on oaths is Jesus' application of the ninth commandment—not to be false witnesses. Our promises are to stand on our own words, nothing else. Write verse 37 in your own words.

4. The use of oaths is a selective attempt we make to give extra weight to some of our commitments. Why is this not appropriate for Jesus' disciples?

Reflect

1. Jesus' teaching on oaths creates a foundation for trust. Think about a person you trust completely. What is the basis for your trust?

2. Consider someone you don't trust. What is there about that person that causes you suspicion?

3. Consider yourself. Imagine you are listening to a conversation between a couple of people who are discussing your trustworthiness. What do you think they would say?

4. The source of our own honest speech is a desire to be pure in heart toward God and everyone else. Picture yourself placing your heart before God. Ask him to wash away motives of self-seeking at the cost of others or God. Write down what happens.

Pray

Pray that God will give you the ability to be honest.

Pray for the church, that we would be witnesses to God's truth.

DAY 13

Resistance

Matthew 5:38-42

But the wisdom that comes from heaven is first of all pure; then peace-loving, considerate, submissive, full of mercy and good fruit, impartial and sincere. Peacemakers who sow in peace raise a harvest of righteousness. (Jas 3:17-18)

There are some who see Jesus' teaching on turning the other cheek as a recipe for living as a wimp. But I don't think so.

My father taught me that I was never to hit anyone unless they hit me first. Sometimes he said it another way, "Never start a fight, but be sure that you finish one."

I've found my father's teaching to be good advice. However, it seems to me that Jesus' teaching is a step beyond the strong advice of my father. Jesus assumes a higher level of strength than my father attributed to me. Following Jesus, I am not to live in fear of defending my rights. When opposition increases, instead of erecting walls to defend my territory, he assumes that I am strong enough to just keep marching ahead. And if painful blows land on me, I don't have to waste my energy thinking about ways to get back at my enemy. As his follower I am to have other resources and other priorities.

Approach

Consider a time when you were injured. Lay your injury before God and allow yourself to hurt. Write down words that describe your pain.

Study

1. Read Matthew 5:38-42. The Old Testament law "an eye for an eye" was God's means of restricting revenge. (The expected response to hurt and pain was to kill your enemy.) How does Jesus' teaching restrict revenge?

2. Jesus tells us not to resist an evil person. List each example Jesus gives, the offense and what is required of the one who is offended.

3. How is what Jesus is asking different from allowing someone to take advantage of you or "being a doormat"?

4. How does Jesus' teaching provide guidance and courage in the task of serving him and advancing the kingdom of heaven in a hostile world?

Reflect

1. Write down times when you have felt offended, hurt or unjustly accused, and wanted to (or perhaps did) respond vengefully.

2. Remember one of these past injuries and replay the situation. This time, in your mind's eye, offer your offender more than is taken from you. Write down your experience.

3. Ask God to show you ways in which defensiveness and fear of being hurt are present in your heart. Spend several minutes in silence, and allow God ample time to bring buried emotional barriers to the surface.

Pray

Ask for God's power to go the extra mile.

Ask that in your church members will choose peace rather than retaliation.

DAY 14

Love

Matthew 5:43-47

The end of a matter is better than its beginning,
and patience is better than pride.
Do not be quickly provoked in your spirit,
for anger resides in the lap of fools. (Eccles 7:8-9)

Before I am willing to marry a couple I meet with them several times. In the premarital counseling, I cover a number of things, from in-laws and finances to sex and communication.

One of the misconceptions I try to expose during my sessions with a couple is the idea that love is always a good feeling. Growing up we often get a romantic picture of love. However, whenever we enter into a serious relationship, we find that those good feelings and positive experiences are accompanied by frustration and pain. I'm not referring to unrequited love or broken romances; I'm talking about the type of love that makes a marriage work.

The apostle Paul writes about such love in 1 Corinthians 13: "Love is patient, love is kind. . . . It is not easily angered, it keeps no record of wrongs."

Making such love work in a marriage is hard. It requires hard work, determination and prayer—lots of it. It is even more amazing, then, that

Jesus requires love, the kind of love that is patient, kind and forgiving, not just toward our lifelong mates, but toward our enemies. How is this humanly possible? It's not. But he still expects it, and provides a way for us to do it.

Approach

Write down things for which God has had to put up with you, ways in which you have chosen to live that are not pleasing to him. After making your list, write down how you feel knowing that he still loves you.

Study

1. Read Matthew 5:43-47. Describe the attitude that Jesus wants his disciples to have toward their enemies.

2. How does the attitude toward those who transgress against us compare with the attitude we should have toward our own transgressions (vv. 29-30)?

3. Ask God to show you ways in which defensiveness and fear of being hurt are present in your heart. Spend several minutes in silence, and allow God ample time to bring buried emotional barriers to the surface.

4. Jesus says that he expects us to be perfect as God in heaven is. What do you think he means by that?

How does that make you feel?

5. From the examples in verse 45 explain how we are to be like God.

Reflect

1. Who would you describe as your enemies? (Consider those who don't like you and would choose to make circumstances difficult for you.)

Why do you think they don't like you?

How does that make you feel?

How do you relate to them on a day-to-day basis?

How will obeying Jesus make a difference in how you relate to them the next time you see them?

2. The love Jesus requires is not humanly possible. It comes as a gift from the heavenly father to those who ask for it. In prayerful reflection consider each person that you have written down; ask God to change your heart so that you really desire his or her good.

Ask God to show you how you could pray for their good. Write down your insights and then pray accordingly.

3. What difference will it make in your church, family and workplace if you take Jesus' teaching to heart?

Pray

Pray that we as God's church would seek to fulfill his command to love our enemies.

DAY 15

Giving

Matthew 6:1-4

If you spend yourselves in behalf of the hungry
and satisfy the needs of the oppressed,
then your light will rise in the darkness,
and your night will become like the noonday.
The LORD will guide you always;
he will satisfy your needs in a sun-scorched land
and will strengthen your frame. (Is 58:10-11)

In today's study, Jesus' sermon takes on a new focus. He teaches about our "acts of righteousness"—what we might describe today as the membership obligations expected of those who join the church.

Several times a year I lead a new members' class at our church. When I compare what we expect at our church with what Jesus expects in his sermon, I think we have made it too complex. It takes us six meetings for two hours each to cover what people need to know.

Jesus' expectations are more simple and brief. He doesn't deal with how much money we are supposed to give, how many times we are supposed to attend church or what committees we are supposed to be on. In his teaching he cuts through our institutional stipulations to the root issue, the exclusive desire to be pleasing to God.

Approach
"Hey Dad, look at this." My sons, like all children, are aggressive in seeking the attention of adults. Unlike busy parents, God is always paying attention to us. The difference is that we are often too busy to notice. Only when we spend enough time with him do we actually discover that he is with us. Sit in silence, until you have given God enough attention to know that he is with you.

What do you experience as you work toward settling in his presence?

Study
1. Read Matthew 6:1-18. What acts of righteousness are mentioned?

2. What are the right and wrong motives for giving money to needy people (vv. 2-4)?

3. Jesus does not discredit the role of reward in charitable giving, rather he refocuses the issue, getting a reward from God. Why are public rewards seemingly more attractive than a heavenly one?

4. How would you characterize Jesus' teaching about God from these verses (vv. 1-4)?

Reflect

1. Jesus mentions giving to the needy as the first of the three "acts of righteousness." What role does giving to needy people occupy in your Christian faith?

2. List as many reasons as you can for charitable giving.

Which reasons seem the most attractive to you?

3. God sees your motives as well as your actions. Picture your heart as a house and ask him to set it right in regard to helping others. After a time of silence in which you allow God to walk through your house, write down your perceptions.

Pray

Pray for needy people in your community, nation and the world.

Ask God to show you how you can help and serve the needy.

DAY 16

Praying (Part One)

Matthew 6:5-8

I waited patiently for the LORD;
he turned to me and heard my cry.
He lifted me out of the slimy pit,
out of the mud and mire. (Ps 40:1-2)

Manipulation and magic are counterfeit expressions of prayer. In all three—manipulation, magic and prayer—we are aware that there is something we lack or that there is a need to be filled. However, manipulation and magic are attempts to exercise power, seeking to get others to do what you want them to do. One casts spiritual spells, the other uses words and contrived circumstances. Both are self-seeking, self-centered and self-satisfying. When directed at people, both are dehumanizing, turning others into objects to satisfy our needs.

In prayer we come to God and ask him to do something for us, get something for us, influence someone for us and in some way meet our needs. The difference is that we exercise no power over God or others in prayer. We come on our knees—poor in spirit, meek and mourning, telling the God of all power what we desire and asking him to act on our behalf. The truly amazing thing is that he often chooses to do as we ask!

We are not above using prayer as a means of power over God to achieve our own ends. Jesus' instruction on prayer cuts through our self-centered manipulation and magic and puts it back into its proper perspective—*communion* and *communication* with God.

Approach

We all have needs. If unmet, unacknowledged or unexpressed, these needs tug and pull at us, distracting us from time with God. Make a list of your needs and lay them before God. Ask him to take them from you and trust him to meet them. Write down how you think he responds to you.

Study

1. Read Matthew 6:5-8. What misconceptions about prayer does Jesus address?

2. What is hypocritical about praying for public effect?

3. Jesus warns against being repetitive in prayer. Why do you think people feel a need to use a lot of words when they pray?

4. If the purpose of prayer is not to give God new information, how does that affect the way we should pray?

Reflect

1. Jesus assumes that prayer is the normal practice of his followers. How satisfied are you with your prayer patterns?

How do you think they could be improved?

2. What do you find difficult about praying to an unseen person?

3. We are to pray, not for public impression, but for divine reward. Ask God to shed light on your motives as you pray. Sit in silence for a while, and then write down your reflections.

Pray

Ask God to strengthen your prayer life.

Pray that a growing hunger for prayer would sweep through the church.

Day 17

Praying (Part Two)

Matthew 6:9-15

O LORD, *hear my prayer,*
listen to my cry for mercy;
in your faithfulness and righteousness
come to my relief. (Ps 143:1)

Writing is not easy. One of the most difficult things for me is facing a blank piece of paper. What terrifying freedom! Until I put something on the page, there is no one who can say whether what I write is right or wrong, good or bad. But in that freedom, there is a gnawing fear. What if I write junk? What if no one understands me? What if I write something about God that is wrong or offensive?

Two things that help me get past my sometimes paralyzing fear are a desire to say things about God and an outline. First, I write about God because the desire to say something about him outweighs my fear. Second, I've found that if I have a clear structure I've thought out ahead of time, then I can risk putting on the page some things that I want to say.

Prayer, I've found, is a lot like writing. I can say anything I want to God. But that is almost paralyzing. What if I say the wrong thing, or say it in the wrong way? How do I know that God will even be concerned with the matters I bring up? After all, he has a whole universe to take care of.

In the Lord's Prayer I have found just the help I need to get beyond my fear. Jesus gives me a pattern of prayer with the right things to pray about in just the right way.

Approach

Prayer is a response to God who is always speaking. We recognize his voice by the help of the Scriptures as we read, study and meditate on them. After sitting quietly for a period, see if Scripture verses that you have previously read or memorized come to mind. Jot them down and tell God you are grateful for his Word and his Spirit.

Study

1. Read Matthew 6:9-15. The prayer divides naturally into two halves—verses 9-10 and verses 11-13. The first half focuses on worship. In your own words, write out the significant words and ideas that it includes.

2. The second half (vv. 11-13) deals with our needs. In your own words, write out the significant words and ideas that it includes.

3. Describe the *attitude* or *tone* of the prayer.

4. How does Jesus' prayer illustrate his instruction on prayer from the preceding section (vv. 5-8).

Reflect

1. If you were to use our Lord's prayer as a guideline for prayer, what changes would it make in the way you pray?

2. Considering verses 12, 14 and 15, we see that forgiveness of others is crucial to prayer. (Remember also the priority of reconciliation in worship from 5:23-24.) Take time now to ask God if there are people you need to forgive. Write out their names and seek God's strength so that you may forgive from the heart.

3. Knowing that our heavenly father is meeting our needs can give us faith to believe that he will hear our prayers. Consider ways that your heavenly father is meeting your needs before you ask.

Pray

Pray the Lord's Prayer for yourself.

Notice the use of the word *our* and *us* throughout the prayer. Pray the Lord's Prayer again and this time focus on other believers.

DAY 18

Fasting

Matthew 6:16-18

While they were worshiping the Lord and fasting, the Holy Spirit said, "Set apart for me Barnabas and Saul for the work to which I have called them." So after they had fasted and prayed, they placed their hands on them and sent them off. (Acts 13:2-3)

Fasting is a neglected but important form of prayer. When we fast, we pray, not only with words and our minds, but our bodies as well.

Like prayer, fasting can be wrongly used as an attempted means of manipulation. Just this past year someone in our city went on a fast to protest the treatment of the poor in our city. He refused to eat until the city council passed a measure that would provide better shelters for people on the street. It was a good cause, and it worked.

However, his fast was not fasting as prayer to God. When we fast, we never hold God hostage to our desires, declaring that we won't eat unless God gives in to our demands. Instead, when we fast, we are saying that we are in need and that his help is more important than our physical needs. As we fast, every hunger pang becomes a reminder that God's help is more important than satisfying our appetites.

Approach

Urgency can be an aid to or an enemy of devotion. Often when we feel driven, we can't focus on God or enjoy his presence. Give your present "fires" to God. Draw a picture of flames representing your urgent situations and ask God to put them out. When you can trust God to handle the flames move on into the rest of your quiet time.

Study

1. Read Matthew 6:16-18. What is Jesus' attitude toward fasting?

Why does Jesus disapprove of it as a public display?

2. There is not a lot of teaching on fasting today. Look up the following verses and write down what you learn about fasting. (Be sure you check out the context of these verses as you look them up.)

Acts 13:2:

Matthew 4:1-2:

2 Chronicles 20:1-4:

2 Samuel 12:15-23:

3. Fasting is the third "act of righteousness" Jesus mentions. In each case he calls for the act of righteousness to be done in secret. How does this compare with Jesus' instructions to his disciples to let their light shine (Mt 5:14-16)?

Reflect

1. What fears or objections to fasting do you have?

2. What would motivate you to fast?

What should motivate you to fast?

3. Ponder wanting God's "reward" so much that you are willing to go without food for an extended period of time. Prayerfully reflect on prayer and write down issues that come to mind. Ask God to prepare your heart to consider fasting.

Pray

Pray that God would release you from any bondage to food that you may have.

Pray for a heart that desires God's approval so much that you can fast, pray or give without caring whether anyone else knows about it.

DAY 19

Rewards

Matthew 6:19-24

Since, then, you have been raised with Christ, set your hearts on things above, where Christ is seated at the right hand of God. Set your minds on things above, not on earthly things. (Col 3:1-2)

Recently, I tried my first venture into the stock market. It didn't turn out so well. I put a small sum in a mutual fund. However, in a couple of months a family need arose, and I pulled it out. The price of the stock had dropped since my initial purchase, so instead of making money, I lost.

Sometime later I was discussing my venture into the stock market with a friend who is a stockbroker. Shaking his head, he commented, "If you are going to make money, you have to leave it in there a long time."

It's the same with our spiritual investments. We can't cash in on all the rewards that God has for us now. It wouldn't be good for us anyway. They are put away for the future.

Instead of discouraging us, that should give us hope. Like those who invest in retirement accounts, as Christians, we can have a sense of security that when the time comes our investments will be there with interest to meet our needs and desires.

Approach

It's hard to have a good conversation when you're sitting on the edge of your chair, waiting to get up and get going. As you begin your quiet time, actually and mentally sit back in your chair. Get comfortable. Tell your muscles to relax, from the top of your head to the tip of your feet. Ask God to take care of your concerns so that you can be free to enjoy being with him. Jot down a few notes about what you like about spending time with him.

Study

1. Read Matthew 6:19-24. According to Jesus, what are the benefits of having treasure in heaven?

2. Consider verses 22-23. These verses about the eye being the lamp of the body may seem difficult to grasp because of cultural differences in the way we think about the way the eye works. Perhaps a good way to grasp what Jesus' point is to paraphrase him, "Be careful what you fill your mind with." Assuming this is a good paraphrase, write out what Jesus wants to teach us.

3. In verse 24 Jesus mentions two masters, God and Money. What power does each have?

Why would a person be attracted to one or the other?

Why can't both be served at the same time?

Reflect

1. Jesus speaks to the values that motivate us. Often these motives are not obvious to us. To the best of your ability, write down the most important desires and concerns in your life.

2. Why is it often difficult for heavenly investments to carry as much weight as earthly ones, let alone be more important?

3. Choose to reflect on God in heaven as your supreme and safe treasure. Bring all other treasures to him and release them. After a time of silent reflection, write down what happened.

Pray

Ask God to make himself the desire of your heart.

Ask God to strengthen your determination to serve him exclusively.

DAY 20

Provisions

Matthew 6:25-34

Come, all you who are thirsty,
come to the waters;
and you who have no money,
come, buy and eat! (Is 55:1)

Before we left for our two years of ministry in England, the promises that Jesus makes in today's study were nice ideas. Now we know they are true.

When we left for England, we put our furniture in storage, took two suitcases a piece, plus Steve's computer, and boarded a plane. We had friends in our ministry organization who provided an initial place to stay and a few possible housing contacts. We quickly discovered that to accommodate a family of five on our ministry budget was going to be difficult. During those initial weeks of looking through the ads, we struggled to trust God.

Despite our doubts, God was gracious to us beyond our expectations. Within a month our needs were met. Both the house and the neighborhood were beyond our expectations, and fit our budget too.

Our return to the U.S. was even more of a faith stretcher. We returned to live with Jackie's dad for our first months back as there were no ministry opportunities when it was time to come back. I struggled to believe that the God who took me and my family across the Atlantic could bring us back again. However, God was gracious. Before the summer was over, there was a call from a church, a home and new friends. . . .

God keeps Jesus' promises to provide for us.

Approach

Home is supposed to be a safe place; you can relax and be yourself. As Christians, we dwell in Christ, he is our home, our safe place. Leave your concerns on the front porch and rest for a few minutes inside the Lord. As concerns come to mind, write them down and put them out the door.

Study

1. Read Matthew 6:25-34. What things does Jesus tell his disciples not to worry about?

2. What is Jesus' attitude toward problems in life?

3. What reasons does Jesus give not to worry?

4. How does Jesus' instruction in these verses on the provisions of life relate to his teaching on prayer in verses 8 and 11?

Reflect

1. What sort of things do you worry about?

2. What will have to change in your life, thought patterns and actions if you are to stop worrying?

3. In quiet reflection place your cares and anxieties before God. Ask God to take them from you. Picture your hands letting go of each care as you place it before God. Write down how you feel and how you believe God is responding to you.

Pray

Ask God to meet your needs and those of your family.

Thank God for the needs that he continually meets.

Ask him to meet the needs of those who don't have food and shelter that you do.

PART 4 *Righteous Results*

DAY 21

Criticism and Discernment

Matthew 7:1-6

Come, my children, listen to me;
I will teach you the fear of the LORD.
Whoever of you loves life
and desires to see many good days,
keep your tongue from evil
and your lips from speaking lies.
Turn from evil and do good;
seek peace and pursue it. (Ps 34:11-14)

As a staff team, we were discussing how to handle the problem of college students who were not keeping to the evening schedule at our conference. One married couple, both staffing the conference, was especially vocal. I remember thinking that they were making fools of themselves by talking too much and too loudly, and were far too dogmatic.

Looking back years later, I see that my sense of silent superiority was fueled by a feeling of competition. I had a few things to say on the subject, but since the couple was dominating the discussion, there was little room for my remarks.

Any time you get people together it is natural to compare, evaluate and criticize. If it is not what someone else is saying, it may be the way they say it, or perhaps how they dress. Whatever the reason for our criticism, Jesus doesn't approve. The fellowship that his followers are to share with each other is to be sustained by standards of humility, not superiority.

Approach

God speaks to us through the events of our lives, the people he places around us, and the issues we have to face. Ponder the past week, jot down words or ideas that come to mind. Ask God to show you what he is saying to you, then write down your perceptions.

Study

1. Read Matthew 7:1-6. How would you describe Jesus' perspective on judgment?

2. Compare these verses with 5:23-24. How is Jesus' approach to judgment similar to his approach for reconciliation?

3. In your own words, summarize Jesus' point in 7:6 as he teaches on pearls, pigs and dogs.

4. Consider verses 3-5. What is the difference between judging a brother and throwing pearls to pigs? (Pigs in Jewish culture refer to those who are outsiders with no interest in God's righteousness. Another way to think about this difficult point is to consider the difference between self-righteousness, prejudice and discernment.)

Reflect

1. Jesus is firm about not judging fellow Christians. In light of this it would be wise to take a personal criticism inventory. What fellow believers are you currently critical of? Write down their initials and why you are upset with them.

Now look at your list. Consider whether there are any traits or actions of those you listed that are present in your own life. Go through each one and underline where you see something of your own shortcomings. This may be difficult. First spend some time in silence seeking for God to give you a glimpse into your own heart. Also ask someone you trust to comment on your perceptions of yourself.

2. Consider your life and the life of fellow Christians in light of the cross. Spend time now reflecting on the cross as God's standard of compassion, both for you and others. Beside the initials of each person you listed, write down the phrase, "I extend the grace of Jesus Christ to you."

Pray

Pray for those you listed. Ask God to bless them.

Pray for the grace of Christ to be shared among all Christians with whom you are in fellowship.

DAY 22

Requests

Matthew 7:7-11

I call on you, O God, for you will answer me;
give ear to me and hear my prayer.
Show the wonder of your great love,
you who save by your right hand
those who take refuge in you from their foes. (Ps 17:6-7)

Prayer is difficult for me. It's not that I don't pray. Or that my prayers aren't answered. But somehow prayer is always slipping lower on my priority list. It gets crowded out behind phone calls, appointments, letters to be read and written, and a thousand other things. I find that I must make new commitments to myself and God every couple of months to put my prayer back where it belongs—at the beginning of my day and the center of my heart.

I used to blame this struggle on my schedule and the pressures of modern life. But I've discovered that that's not it. Even when I am on vacation and my schedule isn't so pressured, prayer slips from first place. When I peer into my heart as to why, I find that I think my success is dependent upon skill and hard work. When I dig a little deeper into my heart, beneath that false pride, I find something else—fear. Maybe

I'm not that important to God. "If I ask, will he listen?"

The emphatic answer both from my experience and more importantly from our Lord in his sermon is "Yes!" God hears our prayers.

Approach

"God help!" needs to be the frequent cry of our hearts. Before we can attend to a study of the Scriptures or give God the worship we want to, we often need to call out for our needs. Don't rush on into the study until you have written out on paper all your needs before God and feel a sense of encouragement that he has heard you.

Study

1. Read Matthew 7:7-11. How does Jesus address our fears that we aren't worthy to have God answer our prayers?

2. How does Jesus address our fears that God doesn't want to answer our prayers?

3. Ask, seek, knock: What do these words convey about the proper attitude of prayer?

Reflect

1. What do you doubt about God that causes you to struggle with confidence in prayer?

2. Our impression of God is conditioned by our relationship with our parents. What is there about your parents that would cause you to doubt that God would answer your prayers?

What is there about your parents that would give you assurance that God will answer your prayers?

3. We often doubt that God will answer our prayers because we don't feel worthy. What can you identify about your character or actions that causes you to fear that God won't answer your prayers?

4. Claim the cross of Christ for your prayer life. Before you ask God for your needs and the needs of others, spend time sitting at the foot of the cross and see the exchange of your sins for Christ's righteousness.

Pray

Pray for your family. Pray that they would know the grace of Christ in the place of their shortcomings and failures.

DAY 23

Standards

Matthew 7:12-14

Come, all you who are thirsty,
come to the waters;
and you who have no money,
come, buy and eat!
Come, buy wine and milk
without money and without cost. (Is 55:1)

There is an exclusive country club opening just down the road from us. You have to know the right people and have a substantial income to be considered for membership. I wonder what it would be like to get an invitation? I wouldn't know because I wasn't asked to join.

No one likes the experience of being left out of an important social function or left off an important social list. However, every social grouping has its standards for membership. Even Jesus has a standard of membership for those who follow him. Anybody who *wants to* can get into his kingdom.

This isn't as easy as it sounds. We might find Jesus' membership requirements a great deal easier if it were left to how much we made and who we knew.

"Want to" is the operative phrase. The requirement for getting in to his kingdom is a strong desire. It's not for the casually committed who act like Christians when it suits their purposes. Membership is for those whose entire life is devoted to walking the path toward heaven, of doing everything humanly possible to keep Jesus' commandments, and who look for a righteousness that transcends that which can be achieved by human effort alone.

Approach

God is always working to get our attention, seeking to draw us away from ourselves to be dependent upon his strength and wisdom. What issues are you facing that remind you that you need God? Write them down and ask God to give you the strength that you need.

Study

1. Read Matthew 7:12-14. Jesus says that the Golden Rule summarizes the Old Testament. List five ways that God requires us to treat cach other well. (For a place to start, consider the Ten Commandments from Exodus 20.)

2. Jesus tells his disciples to enter through the narrow gate. List the contrasts in verses 13 and 14.

3. Jesus' teaching in these verses may feel exclusive. What determines who gets through the narrow gate?

4. Jesus is beginning to conclude his sermon. How does his teaching on the Golden Rule and the narrow gate relate to the rest of the Sermon on the Mount?

Reflect

1. List five ways that you would like others to treat you.

2. Jesus places a choice before us—a difficult journey or an easy journey. What issues (goals) would need to be considered in choosing one or the other (think in terms of the whole Sermon on the Mount)?

3. Picture yourself walking on the wide road. What do you feel like?

What life choices are you making?

Pray

Pray that you might walk more intimately with God as you travel the narrow road.

Pray that others would have a clearer understanding of the two choices that lay before them.

DAY 24

Fruitfulness

Matthew 7:15-20

Blessed is the man
who does not walk in the counsel of the wicked
or stand in the way of sinners. . . .
But his delight is in the law of the LORD*,*
and on his law he meditates day and night.
He is like a tree planted by streams of water,
which yields its fruit in season
and whose leaf does not wither.
Whatever he does prospers. (Ps 1:1-3)

Our two oldest boys are in final exams this week. This means that their study times are more intense as the outcome of their tests will determine their semester grades. We have told the boys we expect good grades. The response we got was, "But, Mom and Dad, you've always said that you weren't concerned with our grades, but on what we are learning. This isn't fair."

Our response was, "We don't want you to study to get good grades, but we expect you to study to learn, and your grades are an indicator of your efforts."

In a similar way, throughout the Sermon on the Mount, Jesus has been teaching about the heart. He speaks to our anger, our lust, and our inner desires for God. Now, as he moves to his conclusion, he says that our outward actions are in fact important because they indicate what is going on in the heart.

Approach

There is within us both a desire for God and a desire to avoid God. Consider ways that you have tried to avoid God recently. Write them down and ask God to draw you to himself.

Study

1. Read Matthew 7:15-20. Jesus warns us about false prophets. From verse 15, what two things can we know about a false prophet?

2. Jesus tells us that although it's difficult, we can recognize a false prophet by his fruit. Using this metaphor, what two points is Jesus making?

3. Keeping in mind that a false prophet would be a religious leader, what might fruit symbolize?

4. What is the end result of a false prophet?

Reflect

1. False prophets offer easy answers to difficult questions and assurance even to those who choose to live in disobedience and sin. Who do you think may be false prophets in today's church?

2. How might a false prophet be dangerous to you?

3. In this passage Jesus teaches that there is an objective standard of truth that is important to a believer. In what ways can you find God's truth?

4. List the fruit that you would like to see mature in your own life.

Pray

Ask that God would reveal his truth to you.

Pray for our church and church leaders in their study of God's Word that they would reveal the truth to us.

DAY 25

Obedience

Matthew 7:21-23

I will instruct you and teach you in the way you should go;
I will counsel you and watch over you.
Do not be like the horse or the mule,
which have no understanding
but must be controlled by bit and bridle
or they will not come to you. (Ps 32:8-9)

In our day there are those who offer miracles as signs of the kingdom. I believe that some of these teachers make good points. Other popular teachers offer self-esteem, success and prosperity as signs. These fruits too may come to those who follow the Lord. Yet while such popular teaching may bring in the curious and needy crowds, they are not the heart of Jesus' message, and they may become distracting idols. Jesus wants us to know that loving him is more important than life itself.

Jesus began his relationship to the first disciples with the words "Follow me." That expectation never changes. If the focus of our life and ministry degenerates into doing things for Jesus rather than fellowship with and obedience to Jesus, then we are in great spiritual danger.

The kingdom of heaven is first and foremost a family. Only those who are in the family by virtue of their continued loving faith in Jesus

Christ, however, are welcomed home.

Approach
God is your heavenly father. Set aside all the things that you are doing for him and enjoy sitting quietly with him. Tell him a few of the reasons you are grateful for his love.

Study
1. Read Matthew 7:21-23. In verse 21, Jesus makes the astonishing statement that all who are known as his followers will not necessarily enter heaven. By what criteria will people enter?

2. On judgment day, some of the actions that were thought to be works of God will not be acceptable. Why do you think he specifically names the acts that are found in verse 22?

3. Consider verse 23. Why aren't their works acceptable to God?

Reflect
1. Picture yourself standing before God's throne at the end of your life. What do you think God will say to you?

2. Obedience to the will of God is the standard by which we are all to be judged. Thankfully, the will of God is to believe in his Son, Jesus Christ. The Gospel of John says it this way, "For my Father's will is that everyone who looks to the Son and believes in him shall have eternal life, and I will raise him up at the last day" (Jn 6:40). Write a summary of what believing in Jesus Christ means to you.

3. The phrase "Lord, Lord" is a Jewish expression of intimacy. What evidence is there that you have a living, close relationship with Jesus Christ?

Pray

Ask God to give you a heart of obedience.

Ask God to lead you into a deeper personal relationship with him.

DAY 26

Foundations
Matthew 7:24-27

"I am the vine; you are the branches. If a man remains in me and I in him, he will bear much fruit; apart from me you can do nothing. If anyone does not remain in me, he is like a branch that is thrown away and withers; such branches are picked up, thrown into the fire and burned." (Jn 15:5-6)

When we moved to Jackson, Mississippi, we discovered that most of the city was build on Yazoo clay. Yazoo clay expands to twice its size because it absorbs an enormous amount of water when it is wet. When it drys out, it shrinks to half its original size. This shifting of the clay causes great stress on the houses and buildings. We were constantly patching cracks in our house. For three months, a door wouldn't close. Then after a rain, it opened and closed just fine. The same went for the windows.

But it could get even worse. There was a danger that under extreme conditions the house could shift off its foundations. The solution to this problem (which most builders wouldn't pay the cost for) was to build the foundation deeper, passing through the Yazoo clay to the bedrock beneath it.

In today's passage Jesus speaks about the ground on which we build our spiritual foundations. Two Christians may look exactly the same. However, the stressful experiences of life will show what they have built their lives upon.

Approach

Think about what you did yesterday. What did you accomplish?

How did you treat others?

How did you interact with God?

Study

1. Read Matthew 7:24-27. How is the wisdom Jesus speaks of related to the rest of the Sermon on the Mount?

2. Jesus speaks of the certainty of coming rain, wind and rising streams. What do these forces of nature symbolize?

3. In this passage what is the sand on which the foolish man builds?

4. What effect would these words have on the disciples and the rest of those who were listening to Jesus as he concludes his Sermon?

Reflect

1. What storms are you currently experiencing?

2. Picture your life as a house with storms beating around it. Take a look at the ground upon which your life is built. How well is it standing up to the storm?

3. Imagine God is doing some foundation work on your house. What changes does he want to make?

Pray

Pray that you would have the strength to act on God's Word.

Ask that God's church would obey his instructions.

CONCLUSION

The Next Step

How was your quiet time?

You have prayed and studied through the Sermon on the Mount. You have practiced the use of the spiritual exercises of silence, study, meditation and prayer. And you have been consistent in focusing on one portion of Scripture for an extended period of time.

These are all important ingredients of a quiet time. But now it's time to step back and consider the purpose of a quiet time—your relationship with God. As you look back over the period of time that you have been working through *Sitting at the Feet of Jesus,* have you sensed that you are meeting with God? Have you enjoyed your times with him?

Perhaps those questions sound a bit too subjective, too feeling oriented. You should know that we are convinced that feelings are an important part of any relationship, and that includes your relationship with God.

Jonathan Edwards, the great American theologian of the eighteenth century, thought that feelings were important in Christian growth. He wrote a book entitled *Religious Affections.* Edwards pointed out that our emotions move us. They are the engines of all human activity. That means that religion that is merely a duty is as good as dead. Without emotions in our relationship to God, we aren't *moved* to God.

So, we ask you again, have you sensed that you were sitting at the feet of Jesus as he taught you through the Sermon on the Mount? Have you felt your heart pulled toward God? Have you found yourself thinking what a profound teacher our Lord Jesus is? Have you experienced the guilt and the cleansing that comes from having your sins exposed by him? Have you felt the pain of mourning and the comfort of his presence? Have you been startled at your worldly desires and stirred by Jesus' promises of divine provision?

The wonderful thing about a relationship with our Lord is that he has not left us alone. He is here with us. He has given his Word and his Spirit to instruct and inspire us. That means that we can learn from him in the Scriptures, and we can live in fellowship with him as we do.

As you continue in your devotions, perhaps with another Spiritual Encounter Guide, or perhaps on your own, we want you to look forward to times of personal encounter with your Lord. That's what makes a good quiet time.